Endless Mothers Love

Author

M Borhan

From

Big 6 Publishing

Mother Grizzly Bear

In the heart of the wilderness, the mother grizzly bear is the epitome of strength and tenderness, guiding her cubs with unwavering love. With each gentle nudge and reassuring rumble, she teaches them the ways of the forest, instilling in them the wisdom passed down through generations. In the safety of their den, she cradles her precious cubs in her arms, their soft fur pressed against her chest as they drift into dreams of adventure. Ever vigilant, she leads them through sun-dappled meadows and shadowed valleys, her keen eyes scanning the landscape for any hint of danger. And as they grow, she watches with pride as they flourish under her care, their bond forged in the timeless embrace of a mother's love amidst the towering pines and whispering streams of the wild.

In the quiet depths of the forest, the mother grizzly bear is a beacon of nurturing warmth and fierce protection. With gentle paws and a watchful gaze, she guides her cubs through the intricacies of their woodland home, teaching them the secrets of survival and the wonders of nature.

In the moonlit nights, she sings lullabies of the wilderness, her deep rumblings soothing her little ones to sleep as they nestle close to her side. Through every challenge and triumph, she is their steadfast companion, a source of comfort and courage in a world of untamed beauty. And as they venture forth into the vast unknown, her love remains a constant, a guiding light in the wilderness that will forever illuminate their path.

However, in the Current story, we are going to discover how the Baby Bear grows fear in the Wild and the Mother Bears altogether removes the fear from their child through constant and unwavering love. The fear of the Baby Bear is a common thing in the wild, and thus the Mother Bear keeps alert for this phenomenon. She removes any hurdles from her child's mind and body through different stages. This is going to be our story ahead, which will read here...

During the Winter Season

Mother Bear cares for the child in the Harsh Winter Environment and manages all for him, from clothes to food.

During the Autumn Season
Mother Bear takes out the Child in the gardens,
while flowers blooming and bees booming

During the Summer Season

The Mother Bear takes the baby in the Greener areas, for having the fresh air and resonance...

During the Spring Season
Mother Bears nourish and look after the Baby Bear, while fathers collect and store food.

Playing in the Sunny Season

The Mother Bear also comes to play with the Baby Bear and the ball in the field and grasses...

Having Summer Fun

In the vast Greenery, the Mother Bear and the Baby Bear have fun together while playing...

After playing a lot in the hot environment, the Mother Bear takes the Baby Bear for a shower...

The Mother Bear washes the Baby
with saaps and Bubbles
by soft and cute hands!
SOAP

Baby Bear's Hydro Phobia
Come Baby, just a little bit just a little
But the Baby Bear is Often frightened to go for a bath, he shivers and doesn't want to go down in the water... Mother Bear is a bit worried

Soon arrives the Christmas, and Baby Bear becomes 1-year-old. But the Mother is always concerned about Baby's Phobia, how could she overcome his fear?

During the Christmas Winter Mother Bear finds way

Mother Bear keeps searching a lot, for finding out
a way to get rid of the fear of her Baby.
Finally, she finds out a way after
searching a lot of books!

Learning to swim
Instead of taking him to a deep river,
Mother Bear takes him to a small spring
She takes her Baby in her lap and arms,
holds him tight, and then lets him move his
legs as he wishes !

Finally Baby Bear can Swim
Day by day, the Baby Bear adjusts to the environment and practice of bathing in deep water reservoires.

After some time, the Baby Bear himself swims
and bath in the Deep water reservoirs...
He also plays
in the water
now

Wow!! That's Great!
Finally, Baby Bear Can swim in Deep reservoirs, Rivers and Sea !!

Yeah, after having full bath, Mother Bear also rubs the towel for getting afresh! That's the power of a mother's love!

Yes! It is only the Mother's endless love that can win Baby's any Phobia Mother Bear's Endless love makes it possible